Best Essential Oils for Dry Skin

Essential Oil Recipes for
Dry Skin
for Diffusers, Roller Bottles,
Inhalers & more.

Rica V. Gadi

Printed in the United States of America

First Printing, 2019

ISBN: 9781690017172

http://eorecipes.net

This book is dedicated to all the strong people who are taking responsibility for your own well being and doing something to be better.

All my heartfelt gratitude to the following people: my mom Ruby Jane, you have made me everything I am today; my dad Nestor-- my eternal, my angel, and the source of my perseverance; Mommyling, my spiritual guide ; Ria & Joe, the true witnesses of my transformation and my foundation pillars; Ellie Jane, the sparkle of our eyes;

Juan, thanks for always encouraging me to push harder - you are my ONE; Rocco & Radha, my reason for everything.

The Love of my family and friends is the fountain of inspiration that never runs dry. Thank you for constantly inspiring me, motivating me, and loving me unconditionally.

This book will never be complete without the help of my trusted and talented friends the #NOWsuperstars and my #oilbularya friends

Blending Essential Oils to use for a very specific reason has become very popular in recent years. There are several reasons why this is so. Blending EOs is basically about inhaling - as it has been proven that aromas have the ability to trigger feelings, emotions and personal memories.

With this in mind, it is obvious that everyone is unique when it comes to what triggers your senses. It all boils down to personal preference for the aroma to trigger what you want to unleash. Everyone is different and we all connect to the aroma differently, so what might work for one might not work for another person.

Of course, we also want the blend we personalize to be therapeutic. This is the best reason why to blend essential oils. We want the blend we create to help us with a very specific emotion or physical conditions. As much as smelling good is important in a blend, it is more important that we blend oils that are not only pleasing to the smell but also produces the therapeutic effect we are after.

Then you have to think about contraindications. Making sure the blend you create is safe to use.

I suggest that before blending, find out if the oils you are using are safe for a condition you may have, for example, if you are pregnant, or have specific allergies. Consult your physician prior to moving forward.

The recipes I have in this book is a compilation of what has proven to work and favored by hundreds of EO enthusiasts. It takes out the guesswork to get you started.

Again, we urge you to read the recipes and make sure that this is safe for you to try.

The book is very specific to a physical and emotional condition. There are several recipes here because you might want to rotate and you may like one and not the other. There are also a variety of applications. Some of us prefer to diffuse, some to make roller bottles, and others to create inhalers and sprays.

I hope you enjoy this compilation, feel free to use the notes section and jot down your fave blends. There is a wonderful world of EO blending - this is just the beginning.

Rica

Dry skin, as the name suggests is when the skin becomes dry and does not get enough moisture. There are plenty of reasons why this can happen and it can range from environmental factors such as dry air, wrong handling of cleaning products such as soap or it can simply be an inherited genetic trait. Dry skin is usually marked by rough, scaly and itchy skin. Severely dry skin can cause cracking as well. It can happen in different parts of the body but it is common to see mainly on our hands, feet, arms, and legs. Exposed skin is more likely to get irritated due to external factors like hot weather, dryness in the air or exposure to certain chemicals.

Dry skin often causes irritation and there are a lot of over-the-counter remedies for simple cases of dry skin. Hand creams and moisturizers are widely used especially in countries with dry climate. A lot of people make home remedies as well, especially if they have naturally dry skin that constantly needs to be moisturized. In most cases, dry skin is nothing to be worried about, especially when it does not show any problematic symptoms that cause irritation. When simple remedies are not able to soothe or cure dry skin, this can mean that it may already be a result of an underlying medical condition.

There are cases wherein dry skin can cause too much irritation and very visible changes. For example, you may start to see red spots, swelling or even blisters. When dry skin becomes too irritable and brings out symptoms like this despite taking simple remedies, it may be time to see the doctor. A medical term for severely dry skin is called dermatitis. It comes in different forms and may be treated in different ways. It is important to seek the help of a dermatologist in order to know what the specific cause of a severe dry skin is so that it is also easier to seek for a remedy.

A more natural way to cure dry skin is by using essential oils. It can be used in several other things but essential oils are known for its soothing and antibacterial properties. It is important to take note that not all types of essential oils can be used for the treatment of all dry skin problems. Different essential oils have different properties and using essential oils in itself needs a certain level of precaution as well before it is taken. It is a liquid with high concentration and more often than not, it should be diluted with a carrier oil before use.

Table of Contents

Best Essential Oils for Dry Skin

Does your skin tend to look flaky or rough? Does it sometimes feel itchy? You may have fine lines or even cracks that accentuate the appearance of aging, particularly on your face. These are all signs of dry skin. And it can occur on your face, arms, legs, or anywhere on your body.

There are many great essential oils for dry skin that work to hydrate and soothe naturally. Find out more about each of those essential oils, plus how to get the best results in this post.

1. Frankincense Essential Oil

Frankincense has wonderful potential for minimizing scars, wrinkles, and fine lines while supporting new skin regeneration. It's very calming and can help reduce inflammation while evening skin tone.

Frankincense has blood-thinning properties; if you have any blood-clotting issues, check with your medical provider before use.

2.Lavender essential oil

Lavender essential oil is one of the most popular essential oils for good reason. It has many benefits for skin health and can help support healing and overall skin health.

Lavender oil is particularly useful for soothing skin issues including rough, dry, irritated skin and may be helpful for reducing scarring.

3. Geranium Essential Oil

Geranium is wonderful for balancing skin, whether it's dry or oily. It's helpful for moisturizing and promoting youthful skin. It has astringent-like properties which mean it may help minimize wrinkles and fine lines and regenerate skin. Its anti-inflammatory properties may help minimize red, dry, irritated skin as well.

Do not use Geranium oil during the first trimester of pregnancy.

4. Myrrh essential oil

Myrrh is another wonderful essential oil for dry skin because it both protects and soothes. It has strong antioxidant properties and may help protect against UV damage while reducing fine lines and wrinkles and supporting youthful skin. Do not use Myrrh essential oil during pregnancy. Use caution if you have diabetes or blood sugar issues as it may lower blood sugar.

5.Helichrysum essential oil

Helichrysum is one of my all-time favorite essential oils for dry skin. My previously dry skin has been much healthier since I started using helichrysum essential oil.

Helichrysum is known for its potential anti-aging and scar reducing benefits because it is very hydrating for the skin. There's also the potential benefit for it to help block UV damage to skin.

While Helichrysum is one of the more expensive essential oils, when compared to the many pricey creams and serums on the market, it can actually be less expensive, especially when considering one bottle of this essential oil can last a long time.

With their anti-inflammatory, antibacterial, and soothing properties, essential oils are used for a variety of skin care concerns. While research into the efficacy of essentials is ongoing, advocates say oils can help dry, oily, and acne-prone skin.

6. Sandalwood Essential Oil

Sandalwood essential oil is derived from the wood and roots of the sandalwood tree, native to Australia, Nepal, and Pakistan. It has a pleasant scent and its antiseptic, anti-inflammatory, softening, soothing, and sedative properties are suitable for dry, itchy skin and conditions such as eczema.

7. Rose Essential Oil

Derived from the Rosa damascena plant or the Damask rose and originating in the Middle East, rose essential oil has antimicrobial and anti-inflammatory properties. It is suitable for soothing dry, itchy skin and refining its texture, including fine lines and wrinkles.

8. Rosemary Essential Oil

Essential oils ideal for dry skin share many of the same characteristics. Rosemary, sourced from the rosemary plant native to the Mediterranean region, has antifungal and antibacterial components. Skin that is dry, itchy, and inflamed can be soothed with the use of rosemary essential oil.

It's also ideal for an itchy scalp and helps with conditions like eczema, psoriasis, and dermatitis. This essential oil is a natural astringent that naturally cleans, tones, and rejuvenates the skin without any of the toxins found in commercial brands.

Before using essential oils, seek input from your dermatologist, especially if you have any underlying conditions like eczema, rosacea, or psoriasis. Stop using essential oils immediately if you experience any negative reactions.

The Blending Process

These EOs are categorized by aromas, and EOs from the same group usually blend fantastically together.

- Floral – Lavender, Geranium, Jasmine
- Woodsy – Pine, Cedarwood
- Earthy – Vetiver, Patchouli
- Herbaceous – Marjoram, Rosemary, Basil
- Minty – Peppermint, Spearmint, Wintergreen
- Medicinal – Eucalyptus, Frankincense, Melaleuca
- Spicy – Pepper, Clove, Cinnamon
- Oriental – Ginger, Patchouli
- Citrus – Wild Orange, Lemon, Lime

Select oils that will give you the health benefits you are looking to remedy. For increased energy choose: Grapefruit, Lemon, Orange, or Citrus. For Calming and Relaxation choose: Lavender, Cedarwood, or Chamomile. You are encouraged to experiment and play with your oils to see which blends work for you.

TIPS:

- Combine Floral EOs with Woodsy, Spicy and Citrus aromas
- Minty EOs with Woodsy, Earthy, Herbaceous and Citrus aromas
- Earthy EOs with Woodsy and Minty aromas
- Citrus EOs with Floral, Woodsy, Minty, Spicy and Oriental aromas

Essential Oils Substitution List

Sometimes we want to blend oils but we just don't have all the oils as stated in a recipe. I've created an easy to use guide for substitution.

Name of Oil	SUB 1	SUB 2	SUB 3
Arborvitae	Melissa	Cedarwood	Patchouli
Basil	Massage Blend	Marjoram	Thyme
Bergamot	Grapefruit	Lime	
Birch	Wintergreen	Cypress	
Black Pepper	Copaiba	Juniper Berry	Clove
Blue Tansy	Roman Chamomile		
Cardamom	Lavender	Clary Sage	Roman Chamomile
Cassia	Cinnamon		
Cedarwood	Arborvitae	Patchouli	Vetiver
Cellular Blend	Frankincense	Thyme	Clove
Cilantro	Coriander	Cardamom	Black Pepper
Cinnamon	Cassia		
Clary Sage	Ylang Ylang		
Clove	Cassia	Cinnamon	
Copaiba	Thyme	Oregano	Clove
Coriander	Lavender	Juniper Berry	Cardamom

Cypress	Douglas Fir	Massage Blend	Copaiba
Detoxification Blend	Geranium	Copaiba	Rosemary
Digestive Blend	Fennel	Peppermint	Ginger
Dill	Bergamot	Lemon	Wild Orange
Douglas Fir	Siberian Fir	Cypress	
Eucalyptus	Respiratory Blend	Melaleuca	Melissa
Frankincense	Cedarwood		
Geranium	Copaiba	Rose	
Ginger	Digestive Blend	Fennel	Geranium
Grapefruit	Bergamot	Lemon	Wild Orange
Helichrysum	Myrrh		
Jasmine	Roman Chamomile	Rose	Ylang Ylang
Juniper Berry	Coriander		
Lavender	Petitgrain	Roman Chamomile	Coriander
Lemon	Wild Orange	Lime	Grapefruit
Lemongrass	Helichrysum	Cilantro	
Marjoram	Basil	Cypress	
Melaleuca	Neroli	Rosemary	Eucalyptus
Melissa	Black Pepper	Eucalyptus	

Metabolic Blend	Ginger	Peppermint	Cinnamon
Myrrh	Sandalwood	Spikenard	
Neroli	Rosemary	Melissa	Melaleuca
Oregano	Thyme	Basil	Copaiba
Patchouli	Vetiver	Focus Blend	Cedarwood
Peppermint	Spearmint		
Petitgrain	Lavender	Wild Orange	Bergamot
Protective Blend	Cinnamon	Clove	Copaiba
Renewing Blend	Bergamot	Juniper Berry	Myrrh
Respiratory Blend	Eucalyptus	Rosemary	Melaleuca
Roman Chamomile	Blue Tansy	Lavender	Focus Blend
Rose	Geranium	Jasmine	Ylang Ylang
Rosemary	Melaleuca	Neroli	Eucalyptus
SandalWood	Cedarwood	Spikenard	Myrrh
Siberian Fir	Douglas Fir	White Fir	Cedarwood
Soothing Blend	Helichrysum	Peppermint	Wintergreen
Spearmint	Peppermint	Reassuring Blend	
Spikenard	Myrrh	Vetiver	Patchouli
Thyme	Oregano	Copaiba	Clove

Vetiver	Patchouli	Spikenard	Cedarwood
White Fir	Siberian Fir	Douglas Fir	
Wild Orange	Tangerine	Lemon	Grapefruit
Wintergreen	Birch	Siberian Fir	
Ylang Ylang	Jasmine	Lavender	

Diffuse

Diffusing Essential Oils is the safest method to enjoy Essential Oils without the risk of an allergic reaction.

Diffusing Essential Oils
Some Tidbits You Need To Know

Our sense of smell is one of our most powerful senses, and as you have noticed in your own experience, some scents affect you more positively in your minds than others. The body contains over 1,000 receptors for smell—way more receptors than for any of our other senses.

Diffusion Essential Oils means the process vaporizes oils into the air by releasing tiny amounts into the air. Inhalation is totally safe and is super low risk. Chances of any EO rising to dangerous levels while diffusion is slim to none.

Diffusing Essential Oils around newborns, babies, young children, pregnant or nursing women, and pets should be done with caution. Read up on safety.

It is advisable that Diffusing Essential Oils for only about 15-30 minutes at a time to be most effective. NEVER leave your diffuser on overnight. Make sure your diffuser is filled with the right amount of water and you understand the operating directions.

While diffusing essential oils, be sure that your space has great ventilation. Crack a window open if the scent becomes strong.

Never add Carrier Oils to your diffuser. This may cause your diffuser to malfunction. Clean your diffuser at least 3 times a week with warm water and natural soap to ensure the diffuser is well maintained and bacteria and mold does not accumulate.

Diffusing Essential Oils
Basic Guidelines

Just a few things you need to know and prepare before getting started Diffusing Essential Oils.

Things you need:
Ultrasonic Oil Diffuser
Essential Oils
Water

Just follow the number of drops in the recipe, drop on to an oil diffuser and fill the rest with water.

All diffusers are different and will have its own water minimum and maximum level. Read the diffuser instruction before use.

Ideally, it is best to diffuse for 15-30 minutes and turn off the diffuser. The effect should be good for at least 2-3 hours. Turn your diffuser back on after 3 hours to reinforce oil diffusing effects.

It is not advisable to use EO in humidifiers.

These are not made to release EOS

Roll

Essential Oil Roller Bottles is the easiest method to enjoy Essential Oils Anywhere and Whenever.

Blending Essential Oils in a Roller Bottle
Some Tidbits You Need To Know

Essential Oils are usually super concentrated and too hard to measure how much to actually put straight from the bottle.

Roller bottles are a way that you are able to create blends ready to use with the right dilution. It allows your EO to last longer.

It also makes it easier to apply exactly where you want to target without getting it all over the place.

It is handy and easy to carry in your purse, ready to use at any time you want to.

I like to apply EOs at the bottom of the feet for many reasons. Our feet have bigger pores than any other skin in our bodies. This means that they are able to suck in the therapeutic compounds in our blend into the bloodstream faster than any other parts of the body. Imagine comparing a normal straw to an oversized straw and how much more you can suck in with the latter. This is how the soles of our feet are compared to the rest of the skin in our bodies.

The skin on our feet is also less sensitive and is designed to withstand some abuse. The risk of having an irritation from EOS is less likely to happen when applied on the feet.

The feet don't have the glands that act as a barrier. Sebaceous glands are glands in our skin that produce an oily substance called Sebum, for the purpose of lubricating and waterproofing the skin. Since this is oil and if you put oil on top of oil, it can act as a barrier or it may slow down penetration.

The feet and palms of our hands are the only skin that don't have these, so it is ideal to apply Essential Oils to the feet for maximum penetration.

Now, it would be hard to apply oils directly and very messy, right? Roller bottles make it super easy and convenient to roll the EOs at the bottom of our feet.

Carrier Oils Info

Carrier oils are vegetable-based oils with their own healing properties that dilute essential oils used to help carry the EOs into the skin.

Essential oils are highly concentrated and could evaporate very quickly. The carrier oil is mixed with the essential oil so it could penetrate the skin before it actually evaporates. Although EOs are oils, it is actually not that oily. When mixed with a carrier oil, it allows you to have more of the essential oil into your skin without wasting EOS to evaporate, making the healing properties of the EO strong and more effective.

There are also Essential oils that are too strong to apply directly to the skin and may cause damage, so it is important to dilute them with carrier oil.

Never add Carrier Oils to your diffuser. This may cause your diffuser to malfunction. Clean your diffuser at least 3 times a week with warm water and natural soap to ensure the diffuser is well maintained and bacteria and mold does not accumulate.

Carrier Oils

There are a lot of different carrier oils that you can use with EOs to dilute them in a roller bottle.

To name a few :

Almond Oil - moisturizing and stays liquid at room temperature. Do not use it if you are allergic to nuts.

Apricot Kernel Oil - moisturizing and suitable for sensitive skin or kids. It is super gentle on the skin.

Avocado Oil - moisturizing and suitable for sensitive and damaged skin. Perfect for skin problems.Can be mixed with other carrier oils

Castor Oil - with antibacterial, antiviral and antifungal properties, use topically to eliminate pain and relieve skin irritation.

Coconut Oil - its antibacterial, antiviral and antifungal properties it is the best and most versatile for skin care. The skin absorbs this very quickly. It solidifies in room temp and may still have a slight coconut oil aroma in it - but you can get fractionated coconut oil to eliminate the 2 challenges above.

Grapeseed Oil - not just for cooking but also great for topical application on the skin.

Jojoba Oil - one of my faves for skin care blends. This oil is the closest to our natural oil our skin produces so it is absorbed easily without being oily. Also amazing for massage oil blends.

Olive Oil - this is the oil for herb type oils. mostly used for cooking but can also be applied to the skin but would need to be blended with a carrier oil that is mild and absorb well with the skin.

Rosehip Seed Oil - super good for deep moisturizing or skin irritations. This oil has a high content of antioxidants and helps remedy dry, scarred and wounded skin.

Recommended Roller Bottle Dilution Guide

RECOMMENDED ROLL-ON BOTTLE DILUTION AMOUNTS

5 ml (1/6 oz.) Roll-on Bottle = ~100 drops (1tsp.)
10 ml (1/3 oz.) Roll-on Bottle = ~200 drops (2 tsp.)
30 ml. (1 oz.) Roll-on Bottle = ~600 drops (6 tsp.)

Roll-on Size	5 ml	10 ml	30 ml	Add EO drops to roll-on, then fill with carrier oil.	
Essential Oil Drops	1	2	6	1%	Dilution Percentage
	2	4	12	2%	
	3	6	18	3%	
	5	10	30	5%	
	10	20	60	10%	
	20	40	120	20%	
	25	50	150	25%	
	50	100	300	50%	

General Guidelines:
Birth to 12 months = .3-.5% dilution
1-5 years = 1.5-3% dilution
6-11 years = 1.5-5% dilution
12-17 years = 1.5-20% dilution
18 years and older = 1.5% dilution-Neat (no dilution)
Elderly or Sensitive Skin = 1-3% dilution
Daily Use = 2-5% dilution
Short Term Use = 10-25% dilution
Local Skin or Systemic Issues = 50% dilution-Neat

These are general guidelines suggestions--not absolute rules--based on traditional aromatheraphy practice.
(Kurt Schnaubelt PhD, Valerie Worwood, Robert Tisserand)

Dilution Basics:

How much you dilute your EO depends on different factors such as weight, sensitivity, health conditions, EOs that are blended in or how long that blend has been used for. There is never an absolute dilution rule, it is you who knows about your level and tolerance. I feel that it is best to start with a higher dilution percentage and increase EO drops over time.

To make sure your EO is safe, make sure that the oils you use are therapeutic grade and do your research on the source and extraction methods used to produce the oils.

Roller Bottle Blending Order

I normally just start with dropping the drops of oil into the **10mL roller bottle**, then adding the carrier oil up until the shoulder of the bottle. Capping the bottle off with the roller and the bottle cap. Instead of shaking the bottle, I like to roll the bottle between my palms first for a minute or 2 for blending, then finishing it off with a few shakes.

NOTE: All recipes in this book are for a 10mL Roller Bottle. If you have a bigger or smaller roller bottle, adjust the number of EO drops based on the size of your bottle.

Inhale

Essential Oil Inhalers are the most convenient way to enjoy Essential Oils Anywhere and Whenever.

Essential Oil Inhalers give you quick and easy access to the vast therapeutic benefits of essential oils.

Blending Essential Oils in an Inhaler
Some Tidbits You Need To Know

EO Inhalers or aroma sticks are compact tubes, with a cotton wick inside and a protective cover, to lock the aroma within.

Your preferred blend of essential oils is absorbed by the cotton wick, and safely enclosed in a tube that fits inside of the cover. The cover is easily removed for access to the tube to breathe in the aroma. Usually lasts about 3 months, depending on the oil blend used.

I absolutely love these because they encourage me to take a moment during super stressful moments, and just breathe.

It is in times of stress when our breathing patterns often change and taking deep breaths promote a feeling of calm and inner peace. Breath work combined with visualization plus a relaxing inhaler, can offer relief to symptoms of stress and help your body to come back to the state of homeostasis.

Aroma Sticks can be carried in your tiny purse, even compact enough to fit in your pocket. You can enjoy your favorite EOs anywhere and you can use them with discretion.

I love diffusing, and do all the time but not everyone in my space may enjoy the scents I enjoy or they may not benefit from the therapeutic benefits of the EOs I am diffusing - so the inhaler is one way to not only enjoy my choice of blends but to keep in personal not affecting everyone else around me.

Inhalers not only benefits me but also keep those around me safe in case the oils I want to blend may pose a risk to those around me who may have a health issue not advised to be exposed to my choice EOs/

When making Aroma Sticks, You may use your chosen EOs at 100% Concentration.

Inhaler Basic Guidelines

Breathe in slow and deep to absorb the EO molecules directly into your olfactory system.

Inhalers are super easy to use. You just remove the cap and inhale from the inhaler tube, count 1 to 5 slowly as you inhale. The EO molecules get drawn into our bloodstream through our nasal cavity and get delivered throughout our entire body.

Simple to use, easy to carry, portable and compact. You never have to be without your favorite blends, ever.

Inhaler Blending Basics

Inhalers are super easy and simple to make.

All you need is an inhaler set which consist of the following:

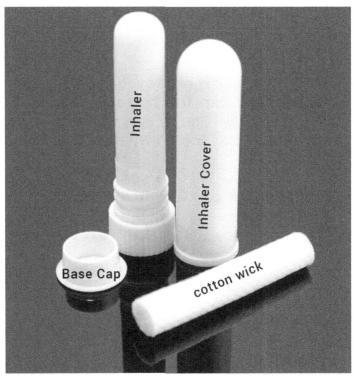

Inhaler, Inhaler Cover, Base Cap and Cotton Wick.

You will need your Essential Oils.

I like to use a pipette for precision and a small petri dish so I can see the oil.

Blending is super easy, just combine the drops and swirl it around in the petri dish and when you are satisfied you can go ahead and drop the cotton wick to absorb all the oil in the dish.

Once the wick is ready you can drop it in the inhaler and cap the bottom with the Base Cap. I usually like to secure the cover with the inhaler so I don't have to do it later.

I usually use 15-20 drops of EO total in a recipe and it can last up to 3 months. Some recipes will need more but on average it is in this range.

Best EO Recipes for Dry Skin

Beeswax Moisturizer

¼ cup Beeswax Pellets
½ cup Coconut Oil
½ cup Olive Oil
10 drops Essential Oil (patchouli, Roman chamomile, vanilla, sandalwood, frankincense, clary sage, lavender, or geranium oil)

Utilize a twofold heater to dissolve the beeswax.
When it liquefies, expel it from the kettle and let it cool.
Include the coconut and olive oils and whip well.
Include the fundamental oil(s).
Whip the blend well until you get a rich surface.
Move the blend to a glass container and store it in a cool and dry spot (don't refrigerate).

Geranium Moisturizer

1 tsp Chamomile Tea (or dried chamomile flowers)
½ cup Water
1 tbsp Lanolin
1 tbsp Beeswax
½ cup Sweet Almond Oil
1 Vitamin A Capsule
1 Vitamin E Capsule
3 drops Geranium Essential Oil

Liquefy the shea spread in a twofold boiler. When it has mellowed, expel it from the warmth.
Include avocado oil and blend.
Include the fundamental oils and whip the blend well until it builds up a velvety surface. Store it in a glass container and use it as your everyday face cream.

Peppermint Moisturizer

3 tbsp Sweet Almond Oil
1 tbsp Avocado Oil
3 tsp Beeswax
2 drops Lavender Essential Oil
2 tbsp Mineral Water
1 drop Peppermint Essential Oil

Dissolve the beeswax and the oils in a twofold kettle.
Warm mineral water (don't bubble) and gradually add it to the liquid beeswax and oil blend.
Continue mixing.
Expel the beeswax from the warmth once it melts and let it chill off.
Include the basic oils and whip vivaciously.
Scoop out the cream into a glass container and store it in a cool, dry spot.
Use it as a multi-day cream.

Myrrh Moisturizer

3 tbsp Shea Butter
1 tsp Vitamin E Oil
1 tsp Aloe Vera Gel
3 tbsp Apricot Seed Oil
5 drops Helichrysum Essential Oil
5 drops Myrrh Essential Oil
3 drops Clary Sage Essential Oil

Liquefy the shea spread in a twofold heater and enable it to chill off a bit.
Whisk the spread once it chills off and includes oils and aloe vera gel. Continue blending.
When it arrives at a smooth consistency, move the cream to a glass compartment. Apply it to your face and body as and when required.

Vanilla Lotion

¼ cup Beeswax Pellets
½ cup Coconut Oil
½ cup Olive Oil
10 drops Essential Oil (patchouli, Roman chamomile, vanilla, sandalwood,frankincense, clary sage, lavender, or geranium oil)

Use a double boiler to soften the beeswax. Once it melts, eliminate it from the boiler and let it cool.
Add the coconut and olive oils and whip well.
Add the necessary oil(s).
Whip the combination properly till you get a creamy texture.
Transfer the combination to a glass jar and keep it in a cool and dry area (do not refrigerate).

Sandalwood Mask

2 tbsp Clay (bentonite, green and white all work)
2 tsp Cornstarch
2 tsp Raw Honey
1 tsp Evening Primrose Oil or Rose-hip Seed oil
1 Egg Yolk
2 drops Rose
2 drops Lavender
2 drops Sandalwood

Mix ingredients together.
Apply to skin and leave on for 15 minutes.
Rinse off with cool water.

Chamomile Body Spray

1 oz Helichrysum Hydrosol
1 oz Rose water Hydrosol
1 oz Chamomile Hydrosol
1 oz Lavender Hydrosol
1 drop Lavender Essential Oil
1 drop Chamomile Essential Oil

Mix all the recipes in a dim, 4-ounce glass spray container.
Splash onto dry skin day and night following purifying.

Chamomile Toner

2 drops Camphor Oil
2 drops Chamomile Oil
1 tbsp Rose Water

Put all the ingredients in a glass bowl and mix them well.
Soak a cotton ball in the toner and gently apply it all over the dry skin on your face and neck.
You can use it once every two weeks to revitalize dry skin.

DIY Hydrating Face Oil

3 tbsp Jojoba oil
1 ½ tbsp Argan oil
2 tsp Rosehip Seed oil
1/4 tsp Vitamin E
4 drops Carrot Seed
8 drops Geranium
2 oz. Dark dropper bottle

Pour all the ingredients into a dropper bottle.
Shake before use.
Cleanse your face. Apply toner.
Gently massage about a ¼ to ½ dropper full

of oil blend onto your face and neck.

Aloe Vera Jelly and Honey Face Mask

2 drops Lavender
1 drop Lemon
1 drop Cypress
2 tbsp Aloe Vera Jelly
1 tbsp Honey

Mix Aloe Vera Jelly and essential oils, then mix with honey.
Apply to the face, avoiding the eye area.
Let it for 15-30 minutes.
Wash off with lukewarm water and pat dry.
Re-apply 2 times a week.

DIY All-Natural Face Oil for Acne-Prone & Oily Skin

3 tbsp Jojoba Oil
1 tsp Tamanu oil
6 drops Lavender
6 drops Frankincense

Add all the ingredients to the dropper bottle.
Put the cap on and shake the bottle.
Apply 4-6 drops to clean, dry skin.

Sugar Face Scrub

2 tsp Sunflower Carrier Oil
3 drops Orange
2 tsp Honey
2 tsp Brown Sugar (more or less for your
desired consistency)

Pour the Sunflower Carrier Oil, Orange and
Honey into a bowl and make sure that it is
well mixed.
Then, add the sugar (keep adding sugar
until the mixture has a consistency that is
gritty enough to scrub your skin, but still wet
enough to apply it easily).
Apply the scrub to a freshly washed face, rub
the scrub all over your face.

Wash off with water and pat dry.

Face Moisturizer for Dry Skin

1 oz Shea Butter
3 oz Avocado Oil
½ oz Sea Buckthorn Oil
1 oz Rosehip Seed Oil
5 drops Lemongrass Oil
10 drops Lavender Oil
6 drops Geranium Oil

Begin with a little warmth safe bowl in a dish of warm water, or utilize a twofold kettle.
Spot the shea spread in the bowl till liquefied. When it mellows, push off from warmth.
Next, include the avocado oil and blend into the shea spread with a fork or spatula.
Mix in the last oils.
Move the finished item to a little holder or container and keep in the ice chest or a cool, dull spot.

Cream for Acne

1/4 cup of Raw Organic Shea Butter
1 tsp of Vitamin C Powder
2 tsp of Rosehip Seed Oil
6 drops of Tea Tree Essential Oil
6 drops of Lavender Essential Oil

Utilizing a twofold heater held only for your corrective needs (not for cooking purposes), warm and liquefy the shea spread until it is melted.
Presently take it off the warmth and once somewhat chilled off, including the remainder of the oils, pursued by the nutrient C powder and blend completely. Empty the blend into a spotless dry 4 oz glass holder, and let it sit medium-term i

the icebox.

Rose Moisturizing Cream

1 cup Shea Butter or Cocoa Butter
½ cup Coconut Oil
½ cup Almond Oil
2 tbsp Vitamin E Oil
6 – 10 drops of Essential Oils

Melt 1 cup butter.
Cool for about 30 minutes.
Mix in almond oil, vitamin E oil, essential oils
(if desired) and coconut oil.

DIY Compress Blend

2 cups Cold Water
2 drops Geranium or Lavender
2 drops Lemon or Myrrh
1 drops Chamomile or Cypress

Blend the ingredients in a container
Add some cold water in a cloth in the
blended ingredients, and wring out.

This is your compress.

Make Your Own Eczema Cream

½ cup Raw Shea Butter
½ cup Coconut or a ¼ Cup Olive or Almond oil
1 tbsp Local Honey
30 drops of Lavender
8 drops of Tea Tree
Optional additions: 5 drops of Geranium and/or Myrrh

Melt shea coconut oil and butter
Add honey and after melting, add the tea tree and lavender.
Combine until it gets frothy and starts to make a lotion.

DIY Symptom Relief Lotion

4 oz Vitamin E Cream
5 drops Carrot Seed
20 drops Lavender
5 drops Geranium
4 drops Bay Leaf

Mix all the ingredients well and apply daily.

Weeping Eczema Cream Blend

¼ cup (60 ml) Shea Butter
15 drops Lavender
15 drops Frankincense
15 drops Myrrh
10 drops Chamomile
1 tsp Vitamin E Cream

Melt the butter in a bowl.
Add scents and vitamin E cream.

Anti-Stress Triggered Eczema

4 drops Roman Chamomile
4 drops Petitgrain
2 drops Ylang-ylang
2 drops Lemon Verbena
6 drops Spearmint
4 tbsp (20 ml) Calendula carrier oil

Mix all the ingredients

Apply gently to affected areas.

DIY Spray for Eczema Relief

8 drops Lavender
2 drops Cypress
4 drops Roman Chamomile
4 drops Myrrh
2 cups Distilled Water

Shake well in a spray bottle.
Keep in a cool dark place for storage.

Your Own EO Blends

Book Ordering

To order your copy / copies of
Best Essential Oils for Dry Skin

please visit: **EOrecipes.net**

You can also check out other titles available.

Bulk Pricing and
Affiliate Programs Available

Printed in Great Britain
by Amazon